B•Y•G•O•N•E

Jesmond Dene

by

Alan Morgan

Published by

Newcastle Libraries & Information
Service

Frontispiece:

A view from Armstrong Bridge, c.1900, towards Jesmond Dene Road. Colman's Field is in the foreground. Stotes Hall is on the upper left.

Acknowledgments:

Many thanks are due to the following for their help with information: Jimmy Donald, Stafford Linsley, Don McGuire, John Yarham.

Much invaluable material has been gleaned from the Newsletters and archives of the Friends of Jesmond Dene.

Photographic acknowledgements:
All photographs are copyright of Newcastle Libraries & Information Service except for no.6 which is copyright of City Repro and no.7 which is copyright of Northumberland County Council.

ISBN: 1 85795 120 4

©Alan Morgan, 1999

City of Newcastle upon Tyne, Education & Libraries Directorate, Newcastle Libraries & Information Service, 1999

Front cover: The Waterfall c.1910

Having acquired most of the present Jesmond Dene by 1862 Sir William Armstrong transformed the semi-industrial and wooded valley, its mills and quarries, into his 'garden', of which the central attraction was to be a spectacular waterfall with stone footbridge, grotto, stepping stones and gorge. The waterfall was created by blasting away the rocky bed of the Ouseburn and then lowering its level downstream between rocks to form a gorge. Further on, dams and weirs were built to provide smooth but attractive stretches of water. A closer look at the rocks alongside the waterfall and gorge reveal sockets used to lift them into position and at the top of the waterfall part of an iron sluice gate remains (although hidden by the people on this c.1910 photograph).

At a cost of around £500 an existing nearby quarry was converted into a 'grotto' or 'rocky pool' by using 'artificial plaster rocks' to make it look deeper and more fashionable for Victorian tastes.

To complete the transformation an attractive footbridge of rock-faced sandstone with a high-centred path and low parapets was built in the early 1860s.

North Lodge is in the background and became in 1883 the first of the Dene cottages built for employees of Newcastle Corporation to look after what had by then become a public park.

For your information …

Copies of photographs which are copyright of Newcastle Libraries & Information Service may be ordered and purchased from the Local Studies Section, Newcastle City Library.

Also by Alan Morgan:

Bygone Shieldfield
Bygone Lower Ouseburn
Bygone Sandyford & Cradlewell
Bygone Jesmond Vale

City Tours visit the City and suburbs during the Summer months. A free brochure is available from the City and Tourist Information Service, Newcastle City Library.

A free brochure detailing other local history publications is also available from Newcastle City Library.

For information on any of the above contact

Publications
City Library
Princess Square
Newcastle upon Tyne
NE99 1DX

or telephone 0191 261 0691 ext. 232.

THREE HUNDRED MILLION YEARS AGO, Britain lay near the Equator with Tyneside a tropical delta where luxuriant swamps flourished and where sands and clays accumulated as they washed down from higher ground to the north. Millions of years later, as the climate changed, more layers were added. The tropical plants fossilised into rich seams of coal, the sandbanks formed sandstone, and the mudflats became shale. These deposits are evident in and around Jesmond Dene.

During the last Ice Age (20,000-12,000 years ago) northern Britain was covered by an ice sheet up to 2,500 feet thick (750m). As the ice began to melt, our present river systems took shape as raging torrents of water gouged their way downhill. It is thought that the Ouseburn originated as one of these post-glacial streams.

The Old English for Ouse is 'yese', meaning 'gushing'. 'Jesmond' has a similar root, being first recorded as 'Gesemue' or mouth of the Ouse, at a time when the township is believed to have reached down to the Tyne for access purposes and a probable salmon fishery.

Bronze Age man is known to have lived in the Dene as in 1844 two graves were uncovered at Craghall. It is also known for certain that a religious house, St Mary's Chapel, existed close to the Ouseburn in the early 12th century with an adjacent spring that became renowned as a national shrine and a magnet for pilgrims.

Industrial processes were taking place in the valley during medieval times. In 1272, as a result of court proceedings, Christiana, widow of Adam of Jesmond, recovered watermills at Heaton (almost certainly on the site of what is now the Old Mill) and Jesmond (probably Jesmond Vale). Other watermills may also have existed at this time, powered by mill races containing water siphoned off from the then fast flowing Ouseburn.

In the 16th century the area near Haddrick's Mill is said to have been the home of outlaws, and, more factually, Thomas Hatherwicke was parish clerk in 1577. Hatherick's Mill occurs in the parish register of 1753. Traditionally the mill became the home of Hendrick or Hadderick, a notorious Danish freebooter and interestingly 'Dirk Hatteraick' in Sir Walter Scott's novel *Guy Mannering* (1815) was a smuggler.

Almost certainly coal would have been dug from the valley sides at an early stage with coal pits appearing from at least the 16th century when they are first recorded in Jesmond. It was considered more convenient to sink fresh pits at short distances apart than to work from one pit for any distance underground. At a later date two important collieries appeared on the fringe of the valley. South Gosforth colliery, opening in 1829 after a frustrating struggle to reach the lower coal seams, celebrated with a candle-lit ball 1,100 ft below ground. The guests all hewed a piece of coal as a memento. The other colliery was located roughly on the site of the present day Fern Avenue.

Sandstone quarrying was another industry carried on in the Dene and some old workings are still visible. The stone was used not only for building but in the production of grindstones for the local mills, and as an export for which Newcastle became famous.

Several farms surrounded the valley and no doubt the need for tools and machines for these industrial and agricultural businesses provided the stimulus for Busy Cottage Ironworks (on the site of the present Pets' Corner) that appears to have been established some time before 1764.

Although 'this fine romantic vale' was still largely undeveloped by the beginning of the 19th century, the well-to-do were finding it increasingly convenient to move away from their town dwellings and build fine country houses either in or on the fringes of the Ouseburn Valley. Landowners were now being tempted to sell off their fields.

Perhaps the best known, if not the first, of these new residents was William George Armstrong, who, as a twenty-five-year-old solicitor, could afford to have 'Jesmond Dean' built in 1835 in preparation for his marriage. The site of his home, which existed for around a century, is now covered by the Glastonbury Grove - Castleton Grove area, though an oak tree planted outside his front door to celebrate the marriage survives along with a stone gatepost nearby.

Always with a strong interest in engineering, Armstrong resigned his solicitor's post in 1847 to concentrate on his newly opened Elswick Works and later, after the artillery problems of the Crimean War, became involved in gun development for which he was ultimately knighted. In a letter to Isambard Kingdom Brunel, the renowned civil engineer who was also attempting to perfect military firing power, Armstrong wrote: 'firing practice takes place between the peaceful hours of 3 and 5 when people are in bed and out of harm's way. The gun is placed in the field where the dungheap was and I fire across the valley against a vertical bank at a distance of 435 yards.' (Not so peaceful for the neighbours!)

As his wealth increased Armstrong acquired chunks of the valley as and when they became available so that by 1862 he was able to enclose as his 'garden' the stretch between Jesmond Dene House at the north end and Benton Bridge to the south. The public were never happy with this arrangement but eventually were allowed access twice weekly on payment of one penny, which was donated to the infirmary.

While the Banqueting Hall was being built in 1862 Lady Armstrong was masterminding the landscaping of the garden, and beginning to transform the uncultivated straggling wilderness into a sophisticated park by creating paths, bridges, dams and weirs, a waterfall and gorge (see the caption to the front cover photograph) as well as introducing many exotic plants, shrubs and trees.

By the 1870s Armstrong was spending more and more time at his Northumberland home, Cragside near Rothbury, where he was developing a new country retreat and indulging in his passion for fishing. By 1883 he had decided to make a gift of his Jesmond 'garden' back to the townspeople of Newcastle, as some were to say 'with compound interest'. He had already donated Armstrong Bridge shortly after its opening in 1878 and Armstrong Park (between Armstrong Bridge and Heaton Park) two years later.

The Prince and Princess of Wales officially opened the 62 acre Jesmond Dene to the public in 1884 with Princess Alexandra planting a Turkey Oak (still there) by the Banqueting Hall. It is said the gardens at Sandringham were later supplied with cuttings from some of the rarer plants at Jesmond. One of the conditions of the gift, insisted on by Sir William, stipulated 'no alterations were to be made to the grounds in a manner to make them more artificial than at present', so much so that the infrastructure has remained largely unaltered since that time.

Following the death of Lady Noble at Jesmond Dene House in 1931, the Dene was extended northwards as far as Dene Bridge (Castles Farm Bridge) and in 1955 an additional pedestrian entrance was created near Parkhead House. A further extension northwards occurred in the 1970s when a pedestrian tunnel through the masonry of Dene Bridge was unblocked following the purchase by Newcastle City Council of land between this bridge and South Gosforth.

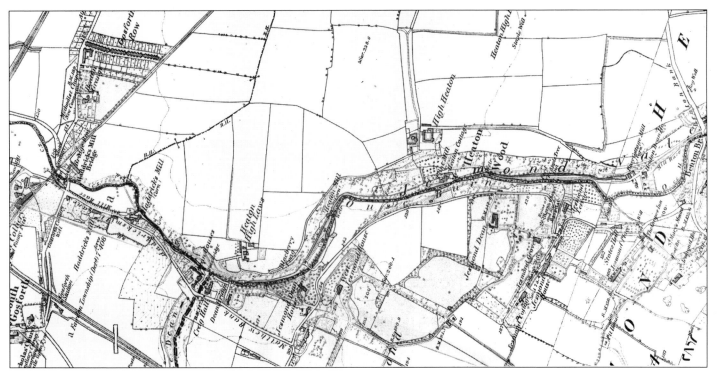

1. Jesmond Dene, for the purpose of this booklet, is defined on this 1862 O.S. map as flanking either side of the Ouseburn between Benton Bridge to the south and Haddrick's Mill Bridge to the north. Many of the surrounding mansions of the wealthy were established by this date and Sir William Armstrong, then living at Jesmond Dean, enclosed as his garden – to public annoyance – the land from Benton Bridge to Jesmond Dene House. Notice the loop in the road near St Mary's Chapel that Sir William decided to bypass in 1871. Other points of interest are the pubs. The Appletree Inn was demolished to make way for the Banqueting Hall and relocated up the hill at a cottage near the entrance to Jesmond Grove (the site is now covered by a residential development). The Grapes Inn, famous for its 'large fruit garden, tea, cider and most delicious fruits in season' was superseded by Orchard House (now the site of Barnardos) and Fenwick Terrace. Busy Cottage Ironworks had become a corn mill by 1862 with Heaton Dene House to the south.

2. An early photograph, c.1900, of Armstrong Bridge, showing the rural nature of Benton Bank and the northern parapet of the lower bridge over the Ouseburn. It is said that Lady Armstrong took pity on horses toiling up Benton Bank, pulling carts laden with coal or market produce and suggested a high level bridge to her husband. A bridge was designed and manufactured at Elswick Works, opened in 1878 and later presented to the borough. An unusual feature were the precautions taken against mining subsidence and heat variations by the inclusion of rocker bearings at the top and bottom of each wrought iron column plus sliding bearings at the central columns to counteract unexpected movement. Motor traffic was stopped in 1963 and after pedestrianisation a regular Sunday market was established. The threat of demolition in the 1970s was avoided, and during the 1980s and 1990s major repairs were made. It is a Grade II listed building.

3. The western approach to Armstrong Bridge and Benton Bank, c.1900. Benton Bank Toll House is on the left, with the chimneys of St Mary's Mount just behind. The toll house was built in the mid-1860s to collect the 'thorough toll', a medieval tax levied on all goods leaving or entering the town to raise money for road maintenance. In 1880 a lease was agreed retrospectively between Lord Armstrong and the Corporation for this toll house for 1000 years at one shilling per year from 1867. The tax was abolished in 1910. St Mary's Mount was referred to in 1828 as a 'snug villa'. It was built for the Rev. Edward Moises, retired head master of the Royal Grammar School, on land belonging to the Hospital of St Mary the Virgin of Westgate Street (hence the house's name), where the school was then based. Both buildings were demolished in the 1960s.

4. High South Lodge at the east end of Armstrong Bridge was one of around five cottages to be constructed at the main entrances to Jesmond Dene after it became a public park. It was built in 1889 and this photograph shows it c.1900. Several of the tenants were Dene gardeners who also had to ensure the gates opened and closed at the regulation times. The large gates (costing, with the pillars, £100) were part of a plan to construct 'a magnificent carriage drive' on the east side of the Ouseburn running the full length of all three parks. A visiting London artist is said 'to have gone into raptures over the picturesque structure', in particular 'the softened red tiles of the cottage harmonised well with the glowing colours of nature'. The lodge has been demolished now, but the gate and pillars remain.

5. Stote's Hall, pictured here in 1910, stood above the Dene, set back from the present day Jesmond Dene Road, nearly opposite the entrance to Collingwood Terrace, where the coachman's cottage still remains. The house dated from 1607, was built for the Gibson family, Newcastle Merchant Adventurers, and was added to greatly over the years, including a top storey. In 1650 it was said to have been the resting place of Oliver Cromwell on his way to Scotland. Later, Sir Richard Stote, a London lawyer, bought the house. Charles Hutton opened a school here in the 18th century, for mathematics and writing, and one of his pupils was John Scott, husband of Bessie Surtees, later Lord Chancellor of England and Lord Eldon. During World War II the house became an Air Raid Precautions depot but ultimately suffered bomb damage when its adjacent lodge was destroyed. Soon afterwards it was demolished and the Dene extended for public access leaving behind only a few trees and traces of garden terracing.

6. Cherry Walk is the name for the old public footpath leading up from the wooden footbridge over the Ouseburn at Pet's Corner (Busy Cottage) to Jesmond Dene Road. It passed Stote's Hall and possibly led to the Grapes Inn, now Fenwick Terrace, with its orchard gardens. Close to Cherry Bridge, shown here in 1971, is a stretch of the river that used to be frequented by swans which unfortunately were harassed by vandals. To try to deter their tormentors, and give the swans more mobility, the water level was raised in 1981 by means of a weir but sadly the last remaining swan was killed in the early 1990s. A small nature reserve of one and a half acres was initiated by the Friends of Jesmond Dene in 1982 on the west side of the Ouseburn, just beyond Cherry Bridge, to provide a safe haven for birds and small mammals.

7. During the 18th and 19th centuries Busy Cottage Ironworks occupied the site of Pets' Corner and Millfield House. It was an ideal location for a forge and foundry. In 1764 the Ironworks were auctioned following a bankruptcy and the advertisement claimed 'the steel furnace (new construction) makes about four tons of steel in nine days'. This billhead of 1833 shows the group of smoking chimneys and buildings, including Heaton Dene House and what became Millfield House as viewed from the west side of the Ouseburn. The Ironworks was run by Robert Rayne and David Burn, each living on site. Their business moved downstream in 1842 to more spacious premises in Ouse Street. By 1855 a corn miller (Richard Davidson) occupied the vacant mill until Sir William Armstrong cleared away all 'the industrial buildings and pig houses' in the 1860s. Later, William Colman, a poultry dealer, lived in Heaton Dene House for over forty years until the building was demolished in the late 1950s (the gate pillars can still be seen at the entrance to Colman's Field). Both stone cottages at the north end of Pets' Corner were built 1857-8.

8. Millfield House, 1926. The first reference to a house here occurs in 1790 when a newspaper advertisement for the sale of Busy Cottage Forge and Foundry adds 'there is a good dwelling house, brew house, cold bath, several houses for workmen and a garden well-planted with fruit trees'. Over the next eighty years the house was occupied by the various owners of the iron foundry and subsequent flour mill. The house first became known as 'Millfield House' in the 1870s during the occupation of Robert G. Hoare, a Newcastle banker. This photograph clearly shows the extension added to the west side at that time by local architect Frank W. Rich. The addition was probably built on the site of old mill workings that included a mill race which flowed from the north (still visible in places) through the garden, exiting down the east side of Colman's Field. Tennis courts, now covered by Pets' Corner, once belonged to Millfield House. Following the death of the last occupant (Miss S. Watts) in the 1980s, the City Council took over the house, eventually fitting it out as a Visitor Centre and restaurant with an archive room for the Friends of Jesmond Dene.

9. By the late 1850s the home of Sir William Armstrong was proving too small and inconvenient for the entertainment of his growing number of business clients. John Dobson, architect, was engaged to design a purpose built Banqueting Hall. The site chosen was, at the time, occupied by the Apple Tree Inn on level ground just above the west bank of the Ouseburn near Armstrong's home. The inn was relocated in Jesmond Grove. In 1862 the building was opened, to be followed by extensions and then by a gatehouse higher up the hillside on Jesmond Dene Road in 1870. This drawing shows the buildings as they would have appeared in the late 19th century. The building featured tall windows and contained many statues. In an anteroom many paintings were displayed alongside a pipe organ powered by water from a pond below what is now Paddy Freeman's lake. In 1883 the buildings and land formed part of the gift to Newcastle corporation. By 1977 substantial repairs became necessary but they were never completed. More recently the roofless and ruinous hall was used as a workshop for stonemasons and woodcarvers. It is a Grade II listed building.

10. Jesmond Dene Terrace, built around the mid-1850s consists of four substantial houses sloping down to the Ouseburn on the south bank of the Moor Crook Letch (a tributary of the Ouseburn). When nearby Jesmond Dene Road was being realigned in 1871 and it was realised that residents would be unable to reach their fresh water supply at a well under St Mary's Chapel, a tunnel was created under the road with a lockable iron gate. A parallel tunnel was also built to enable Sir William Armstrong to reach the Banqueting Hall direct from his home at Jesmond Dean. Well-known residents in the 19th century included the Maling sisters of the famous Maling Pottery family, who lived at number one for nearly thirty years, and Ralph Hedley the artist who lived at number three 1883-1886. This photograph, taken about 1962, shows the south front of the houses and in the distance the twin gables of Parkhead house can be seen.

11. St Mary's Chapel, just off Reid Park Road, is the oldest existing ecclesiastical building in Newcastle upon Tyne, parts of it dating back to the early 12th century. During the 15th century the 'Blessed Mary of Jesmownt' was a recognised national shrine, such as Walsingham, which attracted many pilgrims who were expected to donate a groat. Healing miracles were associated with a nearby well, probably below the east wall of the chancel. After the Dissolution of the Monasteries the Chapel was sold to Newcastle Corporation for £144 and it was then bought by the Brandling family. Other owners followed, using the buildings as a barn and stables. Sir William Armstrong presented the Chapel and an acre of land to the Corporation in 1883. It is a Grade I listed building. This photograph dates from the 1920s and looks from the nave east towards the chancel.

St Mary's Well, inset, lies about 200 metres west of St Mary's Chapel on the infilled Moor Crook Letch burn, beside the site of Jesmond Manor House (part of which can be seen to the rear of this 1920s photograph) and was acquired by the Corporation in 1932. Recent archaeology reveals that the well is not older than the 17th century and that a small 18th century bathing place existed alongside it. The headstone inscription reads 'GRATIA' but may have originally read 'AVE MARIA GRATIA PLENA' (Hail Mary full of grace). It is a Grade II listed building.

12. Left, Red Walk c.1910 with Deep Dene House, now Fisherman's Lodge Restaurant, to the rear, partly hidden from view by the surrounding trees and vegetation. At lower left an old weir on the Ouseburn shows some remaining ironwork of a former sluice that controlled the flow of water to a mill race (visible in places) flowing downstream to the next mill at Busy Cottage.

The photograph above shows the Wishing Well c.1900, on the path just to the right of Red Walk. Many of the Dene's trees date from the mid 19th century when the once natural woodland was supplanted with other varieties as part of Lady Armstrong's landscaping activities. Evergreens including the ubiquitous rhododendron and azalea flank many paths and were presumably introduced to continue the summer greenery throughout the bleak winter months. The Dene continues to be a naturalist's paradise and an urban oasis.

13. A corn mill known as Heaton Cottage once stood on the site of the present Fisherman's Lodge, on the course of a mill race that ran down the east side of the Ouseburn. In the late 1830s the corn mill was converted into a flint mill. This mill would have produced powdered flint for the growing number of potteries in the Lower Ouseburn with much of the flintstone having been imported into the area as ballast from collier ships returning to the Tyne. The flint mill ceased to operate in the late 1850s and the buildings were converted in 1861 into a residence for Andrew Noble, one of Sir William Armstrong's up and coming managers at Elswick Works, and the name changed to Deep Dene. International businessmen wined and dined here. After ten years the Nobles moved upstream to the much grander Jesmond Dene House after which Deep Dene was occupied by a series of businessmen until in 1900 the premises were converted into refreshment rooms. This photograph was taken at the turn of the century.

14. This 1985 view looks north towards the recreation ground, once known as the Maypole Field, close to the waterfall and mill. The brick shelter and toilets, built in the early 1900s were restored in 1982. Two late 19th century bridges cross the Ouseburn here but originally a ford and footbridge connected an old public bridle road (visible on the left of the photograph and still cobbled) which led down from Jesmond Dene Road to the road on the east bank of the river. After Sir William Armstrong purchased this part of the valley he built a footbridge over the public road to allow him access to the northern part of his land, at that time not open to the public. Only the abutments of this bridge remain, now covered in ivy, just visible on the photograph above the left hand end of the arched stone bridge. The path from Armstrong's Jesmond Dean to this now demolished bridge is closed to the public because of ground instability. The other bridge (double arched) in the mid-foreground, formed part of Sir William's plan for a 'commodious carriageway' running the full length of the Dene.

15. The Old Mill c.1890. A watermill, grinding corn for surrounding farms, may have stood here as early as the 13th century. Known as Mabel's Mill in 1739, the next recorded occupants were the Paddy Freeman family, tenants of the Ridleys of Heaton Hall. Part of the family was based at the nearby High Heaton farm. By the mid-1850s flour milling had ceased and in 1857 John Charlton is recorded as the miller, grinding flint into powder for the potteries downstream. From 1862, when Sir William Armstrong finally acquired the valley, all milling stopped with part of the buildings used as a gardener's cottage. Later, the Freemans moved to farms in the Blyth area, and though they never owned land in Heaton their name is remembered in Paddy Freeman's Park, Freeman Road and the Freeman Hospital. The present Old Mill buildings probably date from the early 19th century. This photograph shows the derelict overshot waterwheel together with the end of the mill race (ivy covered) that stretched some 500 metres from a weir and sluice higher up the valley. In 1994 a replacement wheel was fitted. It is a Grade II listed building.

1089.33. *Paddy Freeman's Pond and Lodge, Jesmond Dene*

16. A view of the entrance to Paddy Freeman's Park from Newton Road c.1900. Patrick (Paddy) Freeman and family arrived from Gateshead (Windmill Hills) around 1795 to farm and mill in High Heaton but shortly after 1862, following Sir William Armstrong's enclosure of Jesmond Dene, they moved away. After 1883, North East Lodge was built to house Dene employees at a time when only fields existed beyond the gates. Newton Road (named after Sir Henry William Newton) had only recently opened to allow access to Gosforth colliery from Heaton. In 1928 that part of the road alongside the park was renamed Freeman Road. Paddy Freeman's lake originated as a duck pond attached to their High Heaton farm immediately to the right of this photograph. The pond was enlarged to its present size and made user-friendly c.1890. To the left of the photograph an island in the lake is visible which was later removed. The farm buildings were demolished between the wars as a prelude to surrounding residential development and for many years High Heaton Tennis Club occupied the site, until Anscomb Gardens was built in the 1960s.

STEPPING STONES, JESMOND DENE, NEWCASTLE

17. The Stepping Stones, a short distance upstream from the waterfall, were another of Sir William Armstrong's 'improvements' of the 1860s. This photograph, taken c.1900, looks north, with North Lodge just out of sight on the right. The bridge across the Ouseburn was built in 1889 as part of the 'commodious carriageway' scheme from Armstrong Bridge to Matthew Bank which formed the northern boundary of Jesmond Dene until after Lady Noble died in 1931. A similar carriageway already ran through Heaton and Armstrong Parks. Beyond the bridge on the right (not visible on this photograph) is the remains of an old quarry known as Blaeberry Crag, said to be the source of grindstones, much exported from Newcastle. Sir William Armstrong converted the quarry into an oriental garden, where no doubt much 'far eastern' business took place. Today high sandstone cliffs, occasionally used by rock climbers, dominate an area of wild plants, shrubs and trees.

18. The first house built on this site was 'Black Dene,' designed in 1822 by John Dobson for Dr Thomas E. Headlam, a Newcastle physician. In 1851 Dobson redesigned the building for William Cruddas (a family connected with Elswick Works) and it became known as Jesmond Dene House. Andrew Noble moved here in 1871 and Norman Shaw (architect of Cragside near Rothbury) enlarged the premises (almost obliterating Dobson's house). In 1896, as Elswick Works flourished and notable guests needed to be housed, local architect Frank Rich rebuilt the property into a 39-roomed mansion. Many distinguished guests stayed here including de Havilland (the aircraft designer), Rudyard Kipling and Baden Powell. After Lady Noble's death in 1931 Newcastle Corporation took over the house. During World War II it was used by Air Raid Precautions and after the war as a hostel for local workers. This photograph, which shows the variety of architecture, was taken in 1964 when it was used as a Special School.

19. Dr Headlam built Dene Bridge in 1850 to give access to Matthew Bank from Heaton High Laws Farm (now Castles Farm) avoiding a route round his home at Black Dene (later Jesmond Dene House). Headlam owned virtually all the surrounding land. This 1960s photograph looks north towards the single-track bridge. There are commemorative stone plaques on the outside parapets. The buildings of Heaton High Laws Farm originated as three late 18th century follies later converted into a farmhouse with two outbuildings. In the 1860s five cottages were added and around ten years later it had become known as 'Three Castles Farm'. Further residential developments occurred in the 1980s.

The large brick building on the opposite side of the Ouseburn was designed as a Raquet Court for Sir Andrew Noble of Jesmond Dene House, a keen player of Real Tennis. It was one of only seven courts in England when it opened in 1894. Noble engaged a full-time professional coach, provided him with a house attached to the court, and continued playing this vigorous game (a mixture of tennis and squash) into his eighties.

20. Craghall was formerly a short row of stone-built cottages on the bank of the Craghall Burn, built for miners of the nearby pit and said to date from 1788. Conversion into a dwelling for Dr Headlam (who later moved to the nearby Black Dene) took place in 1814. The Craghall Burn once formed the boundary between Jesmond and South Gosforth. In 1893-94 the upper part was culverted and infilled with spoil from the railway widening programme. Charles Murray Adamson, a Newcastle solicitor, settled here in 1846, the family remaining until 1930. Hugh Wood, the local mining engineer, lived here in the 1940s. Following the threat of demolition in the 1970s, when this photograph was taken, the property became a divisional office of the Northumbrian Water Authority and from 1982 a home for the elderly.